# Dance STANCE

## BEGINNING BALLET FOR YOUNG DANCERS

ONCE UPON A
Dance

Ballerina Konora - Teacher Terrel - Stella Maris

# Also by Once Upon a Dance

Dedicated to
Eva for the choreography,
Andrea for the jam,
Peter for the wisdom,
Michelle, our weight-shift expert,
and all the teachers who helped my dance stance, especially
at Emerald Ballet Academy and Pacific Northwest Ballet.

Dance Stance: Beginning Ballet for Young Dancers with Ballerina Konora
(Ballet Inspiration and Choreography Concepts for Young Dancers Series)

© 2022 ONCE UPON A DANCE

Illustrated by Stella Maris Mongodi, www.stellamarisart.it
Layout and cover design by Stella Maris Mongodi
Author/Publisher: Once Upon a Dance
Ballerina Konora Photo @heidialhadeffleonard

All proceeds donated to charity.

LCCN: 2022904395
ISBN: 978-1-955555-227; 978-1-955555-234; 978-1-955555-241
    (paperback)    (ebook)    (hardcover)

Juvenile Nonfiction: Performing Arts: Dance
(Juvenile Nonfiction: Concepts: Body; Juvenile Nonfiction: Careers)

First Edition

# WHAT'S THIS BOOK ABOUT?

gourmand cat

more advanced stuff

dance
stance

Hello Fellow Dancer,

Thanks for joining me for some "dance stance" practice!

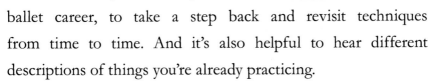

I've found it helpful, over my ballet career, to take a step back and revisit techniques from time to time. And it's also helpful to hear different descriptions of things you're already practicing.

I like to think of dance as a **gorgeous multi-layered cake,** full of delicious fillings such as jam and cream. It's beautifully decorated with icing and swirls. All of the different ingredients work together to make a wonderful cake that everyone can enjoy.

The **first layer of the dance cake is posture** and that's what we will learn about in this book. The book is not meant to be a substitute for in-person training, which will be necessary if you want to pursue dance seriously. I also want to note that not all ballet styles agree with the fundamental advice here. For example, the Cecchetti method, in particular, would say something quite different.

I've added my "Notes from a Ballerina" diary pages in case you want to come back to those later.

*Konora*

# I

# WHAT'S A "DANCE STANCE" ANYWAY?

I am a graceful ballerina who loves to dance. I've practiced for many, many years to become an expert dancer.

Ballet builds step by step. When a professional dancer performs a ballet move on stage, it represents years of practicing ever-harder steps. We dancers study the building blocks of ballet, creating taller towers of skills with each passing year.

9

One of the first building blocks, which we continue working on for years or even decades, is how to stand. Let's call this our "dance stance." It's the basis of everything.

Creating good posture and thinking about where we place our feet and how we connect to the floor allows us to balance, spin, and jump.

So, how do we find our dance stance? Let's start at the beginning, which is always a good place to start.

# 2

# THIS IS WHERE YOU NEED A LOT OF IMAGINATION

Stand with your toes facing forward and your feet parallel like two railroad tracks.

Bring your toes together just a smidge with a little more space between your heels than between your toes. Imagine spreading the soles and toes of your feet out across the floor, as if you wanted your feet to touch the edges of the room.

Or perhaps imagine you have wide duck feet and long frog toes. Try to feel you are attached to the earth. You are grounded and secure, like a magnet attached to metal.

Now, gently press your toes into the floor. Notice the way your whole body adjusts and tilts forward. We've shifted our weight forward into our toes. Pretend you're standing on sand and want to leave a perfectly even footprint, with the toes showing as much as the heel.

Next, push harder into the floor with your evenly spread feet. Perhaps you are a tree, and your roots reach into the ground, searching for water deep below the surface. You might notice you feel a little taller, and that's great!

Close your eyes and let your spine—the set of bones that run down the length of your back—grow even longer.

Imagine you have a glass of water on your head and you don't want to spill it. This helps to keep your head straight.

Then, think about widening your shoulders out to the sides, reaching them into the surrounding space.

Sometimes I like to imagine I have peacock feathers, or I'm a cobra snake stretching my hood sideways and flattening out my snake neck.

See if you can take a deep breath into your belly while keeping your tall, wide shape.

Last step for now: pull your belly button up and back toward your spine, almost as if you're zipping up a pair of pants.

Think of your tailbone, the bottom of your spine, as a heavy, solid weight, dropping toward the ground. The pull of this feeling, against the glass of water on your head, should feel dynamic, as if there's lightning racing around inside of you.

This keeps you activated, like a superhero who's already in their super suit, ready to defend the world.

Phew! Enough. Relax. Was that hard work? If the answer is yes, fantastic—that means you were working your muscles in a new way. Of course, they shouldn't feel painful, only a little tired or a bit achy.

# 3

# UP A NOTCH
## (ALREADY??!)

When you're ready for another try, we can add turnout, which is the rotation of our legs.

Moving back into your dance stance, shift your weight back into your heels—the bottom part at the back of your feet—so that your toes can easily slide open and closed.

Try moving the toes of both feet apart, then bring them together again. Are your heels still together?

Do this a few times. Focus on your tall straight back, your wide open shoulders, and that steady glass of water on your head.

Using almost the same movement as before, rock back onto your heels a little more so that your toes can lift up in the air. While keeping your dance stance and your legs straight, rotate the whole of both legs outward as far as you can, then plop your toes down again. That's your first position.

There's so much effort required just to dance stance, right? Great work getting this far. You should pat yourself on the back for making your posture a priority.

If you want a movement break, I've left some Notes from a Ballerina for you. Or if you're in the groove, you can come back to those nuggets of wisdom later.

# DANCE BEING STILL. SO WEIRD.
## (NOTES FROM A BALLERINA 1)

Choreographers—dance creators—use standing and stillness when they create dances. Movement is exciting, but stillness can be just as dramatic!

While I was training at Pacific Northwest Ballet, one of my favorite teachers incorporated a lot of choreography and improvisation—moving without a planned sequence of steps. I loved the opportunity to make dances and move in my own way.

One day, she asked us to create a brief dance and add moments of stillness. The first group performed their dance and had a couple of pauses of about the amount of time I was planning to use. I thought it looked great.

Then our teacher had the group show the same dance but tripling the time of each pause. I was thinking, "Wow, this is going to be super boring! We have to watch a bunch of statues for thirty seconds at a time?"

Boy, was I wrong! It was so interesting and unexpected to have those looongggggg pauses in the dance. Lesson learned!

# DEFINING DANCE

## (NOTES FROM A BALLERINA 2)

Everyone has different ideas about what defines dance. What do you think?

There's a frequent discussion in my family that goes, "But was it dance?"

My mom likes her dance performances to have dance moves, but choreographers sometimes decide that dance is more interesting when it includes things that many people don't consider dance.

I've seen performances with extreme moments of stillness, and sometimes with a great deal of standing or other poses. One show even had a person on stage in the same exact pose for the entire performance.

It's amazing how a person's energy or presence can create powerful feelings and moods, even when they are hardly moving.

As a performer, it's certainly worth remembering that someone can capture the audience's attention and admiration with little or no movement.

My mom might disagree, which is a great reminder that we all have different opinions, and that dance is subjective, meaning people react based on their previous experiences, ideas, and preferences.

# 4

# BECOMING A FLAMINGO

While there's occasionally a standing-only role, you probably already know that most ballet is accomplished with one leg in the air, sometimes even two legs in the air as we jump and leap across the stage.

Before we lift a leg in the air, let's experiment a bit more with weight shift. This will help us stand on one foot without falling over.

Let's go back to parallel with our knees and toes facing front, finding our dance stance. Pretend there's a tiny string attached to your hip bone. To find your hip bone, reach your elbows to the side and put your hands on your hips with your curled fingers forward and thumb behind. Your hip bones will be near your fingertips.

In your imagination, pull this string sideways and bring your whole body—especially the top half—with you as you shift your weight over to one side. Keep that imaginary water glass balanced on your head!

Now shift back to the center, and continue moving your weight over to the other side. Just keep shifting back and forth, and when you are ready, go faster. Keep pressing the toes into the floor so the weight's distributed across the toes and heel on each foot. You can think of each leg as a separate camera tripod: two supports run down the front of each of your legs, while the third tripod support is in the back, reaching into the center of each heel.

As you shift side to side, does it feel like you could lift one foot off the floor? If so, keep thinking about your dance stance as you lift up one leg.

# LOOK MA, NO HANDS!
## (NOTES FROM A BALLERINA 3)

A few tips and tricks to improve your balance:

- It's tempting to clench or grip your muscles when you are trying to hold on to a balance, but the opposite is more helpful. Imagine your energy expanding in every direction: to the sides, out of the top of your head, and reaching into the ground.

- Now, imagine trying to touch something with the top of your head or pushing the floor away to find even more stabilizing energy.

- Creating a visual image such as the roots of a tree reaching into the ground, the magnet on metal, the frog toes and duck feet, or even simply picturing yourself steady and stable can help.

- Practice your balance with your eyes closed. It's not easy, but it will help you feel the structure in your body.

- Engage your core (your belly!) by zipping up your imaginary pants zipper.

# 5

# RELE–MEH

Let's shift back to the center, feeling all six of those tripod contacts holding equal weight. Now, still in parallel, slowly lift your heels up and press into those two front supporting tripod legs.

When you rise to your toes from your flat foot in ballet dancing, it's called relevé (but I call it *rele-meh*, sometimes, when I'm disappointed).

Imagine having a nail between your front two toes and a ball between your ankles to help connect you to the floor and keep an ideal foot position. If you feel your shoulders fall back or your belly move forward, try it again and imagine zippers are zipped up both sides of your legs and all the way to your shoulders.

You can also pretend you're leaning forward to smell a gigantic pot of your favorite food, but you can barely move for fear of touching the hot pot.

If that feels good, try shifting your weight a little while you are up on tiptoes. Think of a string pulling you just a bit over to one side while keeping your upper body aligned, as if you are balancing your hips-chest-head tower. Standing on one foot in relevé will take a lot of practice, but eventually you might be ready to lift a leg from this position.

Come down, relax, and shake out your feet and legs. When you're ready, try a relevé with your legs turned out.

Pull your heels forward, and keep pulling them forward as you lift them off the floor. Imagine a rubber band attached to each heel that keeps your heels facing each other.

It will take some effort to keep your upper body still as you come up in first position relevé. If you lean back or lose your dance stance, try pushing your big toes into the floor.

When you're ready, try a weight shift in this rotated relevé.

Are your calf muscles all right? Don't stay up there very long if this is your first time doing relevés.

Relax and shake it out again.

Weight in
your big
toe!

42

# ADVICE FOR YOUR FUTURE OLDER SELF
## (NOTES FROM A BALLERINA 4)

- Good posture is good for you in dance and in life. It strengthens your core and prevents injury. Even if you never dance again, you could use this posture.

- Standing (and sitting) taller and nicely stacked up in your personal tower gives you more space to breathe, which gives your body more oxygen. Good posture keeps your core muscles working, which helps stabilize you. A strong core means you're less likely to injure your back or lose your balance and fall.

- I've learned to be more aware of my posture throughout my daily life, and it's made me a better dancer. As you go through your day, think about holding this stance, and it will strengthen your body.

# 6

# DANCE STANCE IS A GIRL'S BEST FRIEND

A lot of our dance training is about moving while keeping our dance stance. We do our pliés (our knee bends), our tendus (reaching one leg out), and our passés (one of many positions on one leg) while we focus on our dance stance.

These moves and other steps we practice in class both warm up our muscles and help us prepare for more complicated dance steps.

Whaaat

Pas de bourrée
Developpé Pas de chat
Battlement tendu Arabesque
Chassé Grand jeté Port de bras

# EVERYBODY STINKS AT FIRST
## (NOTES FROM A BALLERINA 5)

Do you know what I've learned over the years? Hardly anyone likes ballet during their first year. There's so much to think about, it can all feel a bit overwhelming.

Just when you have your dance stance figured out, the teacher adds more movements—and not just one or two, but whole sequences of steps.

Then there are all those new words, which can be so confusing.

How does anyone remember all this stuff?

# PRACTICE MAKES PURRFECT
## (OR AT LEAST BETTER. WHO'S PERFECT, AFTER ALL?)

The harder something is, the further you'll come. Here's the big secret: practice makes everything better. I think ballet is so rewarding, in part, because it isn't easy.

I've seen people come into class and not even know how to turn their toes in the right direction. As they put the time and effort in, they see themselves improve and feel excited because they recognize how far they've come.

If you stick with it, there's so much to learn and your progress will be obvious. Plus, jumping and turning are pretty cool!

Everything was so hard

but then I saw I improved

50

# IT'S OK TO TAKE A BREAK
## (I DID TOO)

Ballet doesn't have to be all or nothing. Why do we all think we have to stop altogether?

I had danced most of my life, but stopped when I was around ten years old. The place where I was studying wanted more commitment, but I wanted time for other things. Everyone except me took multiple classes, and I ended up feeling left behind. I stopped taking classes for a year before deciding to give ballet another chance.

Kids who are busy trying other new activities must often commit to taking ballet three times a week. It can feel like ballet is all or nothing, which I think is unfortunate.

# 70 AND STILL ROCKIN'
## (IT'S NEVER TOO LATE TO LEARN NEW SKILLS)

Even adults can learn ballet. Because many dance studios ask for greater commitment and increased class time every year when students are young, many kids drop out of ballet along the way. Adults often come back to it later in life, when they finally realize they can take ballet classes once or twice a week, and that it doesn't have to be so life-consuming.

You can even learn ballet for the first time as an adult. My mom teaches ballet, and she has a group of women who started learning as older adults (and she's also taught men). The group calls themselves the Sisterhood of the Pink Tights, and most of them are over seventy years old! The Sisterhood of the Pink Tights is an inspiration. They remind us all that you can keep learning new skills and making new friends all your life. That's what makes life interesting and worth living.

The Pink Tights and Friends

53

# CURIOSITY DOESN'T ALWAYS KILL THE CAT!
## (POOR CAT)

Seek new experiences and ideas to find inspiration as a dancer.

I hope you have a life rich with new opportunities.

Dancers get a lot of advice from their teachers. Some of the best advice I've ever heard is that to be a truly creative dancer or choreographer, one must find inspiration through experience: trying new things, connecting with new people, and seeking new ideas in books, art, performances, movies, and nature.

# ENJOY THE RIDE
## (IT CAN BE A ROLLERCOASTER)

The journey is just as important as the destination!

When I was fourteen, I tore my hamstring (a muscle in my leg) just before a show. I wasn't able to perform (or even walk). My mom said she was sorry that I had to miss the big event, something I'd been working toward for so many months.

I told her the show wasn't everything. Just as important was the process: being with my friends, learning the choreography, and improving my skills.

I surprised myself with this wisdom! Today, I still try to find joy in learning, like my wise, younger self.

# AND ABOVE ALL...

### Have fun!

- Remember, everything is hard in the beginning.
- Be kind and patient with yourself as you tackle new challenges, explore new ideas, and enjoy different experiences.
- Find joy in your learning.
- And perhaps most importantly,
    remember to have fun along the way.

Until our next dancing adventure,
    Love,
        *Konora*

🐾 Kittina

# Thee End

THE END

(WE END OUR STORIES THIS WAY
IN HONOR OF MY GRANDPA.)

# WE'D LIKE TO CONNECT!

We are a mother-daughter pair, both happily immersed in the ballet world until March 2020. With an initial plan to publish one book, ONCE UPON A DANCE has published 25 books with the mission to keep kids moving at home during the pandemic.

The greatest challenge is getting the books in the hands of kids who will enjoy them. With this goal in mind, we donate *Dance-It-Out! Creative Movement Stories* to libraries, dance instructors, and teachers—if you know someone in this category, please send them our way.

In the meantime, we check for reviews daily, and we'd be immensely grateful for a kind, honest review from a grown-up on Amazon or Goodreads or a shout-out or follow on social media if you enjoy our books.

@Once_UponADance (Instagram)
OnceUponADanceViralDancing (Facebook)

ONCE UPON A

www.ONCE UPON A DANCE.com

WATCH FOR SUBSCRIBER BONUS CONTENT

# DANCE–IT–OUT!
## COLLECTION FOR AGES 4+

# DANCING SHAPES
## COLLECTION FOR AGES 6+

## COMING SOON:
## DANCING SHAPES WITH CATS

Made in United States
Orlando, FL
17 October 2022

23529312R00035